WOMEN SONGWRITERS HALL OF FAME
WSHOF

THE THEME OF THE AWARD SHOW IS

LEGENDS, LUXE & LYRICS

ATTIRE? BLACK TIE & OVER THE TOP!

Union Station – 50 Massachusetts Ave NE
Washington DC, 20002

TICKETS
www.womensongwritershalloffame.org

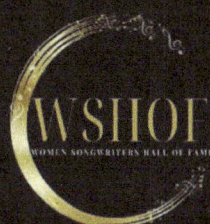

Pump it up Magazine

TABLE OF CONTENTS

⚡ EDITORIAL
Page 5

⚡ ALYZE ELYSE
A Journey of Creative Success & Women Songwriters Hall of Fame INDUCTION

6

⚡ WHAT'S HOT
- Review:
Are You in Paine?
Discover the healing power of music frequency
Best Indei Songs
- Women Empowering
Music Books and Movies

⚡ BEAUTY
- Top tips to stay young

10

⚡ FASHION
Top Tips
to look younger

⚡ FITNESS - WELLNES
- Couple's Workouts
- Crosswords: Expert Tips for Mental Health

21

⚡ TOP TIPS
- Live Stream Success!

⚡ Puzzles and Games!
Have Fun!

27

⚡ HUMANITARIAN AWARENESS
Overcoming Anxiety

Pump it up
MAGAZINE ®

PUMP IT UP MAGAZINE

LINKS

WEBSITE
www.pumpitupmagazine.com

FACEBOOK
www.facebook.com/pumpitupmagazine

TWITTER
www.twitter.com/pumpitupmag

SOUNDCLOUD
www.soundcloud.com/pumpitupmagazine

INSTAGRAM
pumpitupmagazine

PINTEREST
www.pinterest.com/pumpitupmagazine

PUMP IT UP MAGAZINE
30721 Russell Ranch Road
Suite 140
Westlake Village,
California 91362
United States

 (818)514 – 0038(Ext:102)
 info@pumpitupmagazine.com

EDITORIAL

Dear Readers,

Welcome to the latest issue of Pump It Up Magazine! We are thrilled to share with you an extraordinary journey of talent, passion, and achievement.

This month, we shine the spotlight on Alyze Elyse, a true powerhouse in the entertainment industry and a proud inductee into the Women Songwriters Hall of Fame.

Alyze Elyse is a name that resonates with creativity and success. As a screenwriter, songwriter, filmmaker, and actress, Alyze has left an indelible mark on multiple artistic disciplines. Her remarkable journey is an inspiration to all women and aspiring artists, demonstrating the transformative power of perseverance, dedication, and raw talent.

Within the pages of this issue, we delve into the life and accomplishments of Alyze Elyse, uncovering the challenges she faced and the triumphs she celebrated along the way.

Her induction into the Women Songwriters Hall of Fame stands as a testament to her exceptional contributions to the music industry and her influence as a female artist.

In addition to Alyze's incredible story, we have curated a wide range of content to captivate and empower you.

Discover our exclusive fashion and beauty tips to stay and look young. Enhance your natural beauty, embrace your radiance, and let your inner glow shine brightly!

Also, don't miss our captivating content on fitness, mental health, and empowering yourself through music, movies, books, and crosswords. Discover new ways to enhance your well-being and fuel your passion for art and culture!

We extend our gratitude to all our readers and contributors for being a part of the Pump It Up Magazine community. Together, let's celebrate the remarkable accomplishments of Alyze Elyse, amplify the voices of women songwriters, and empower each other to embrace our creativity.

Follow us @PUMPITUPMAGAZINE and visit our website www.pumpitupmagazine.com to stay connected with our vibrant community and be the first to know about our upcoming issues, featuring more incredible talents and inspiring stories.

Tune in to WWW.KPIURADIO.COM - THE WEST COAST WAVE - PUMP IT UP MAGAZINE OFFICIAL RADIO STATION!

Pump It Up Magazine - where creativity flourish!

With warmest regards,

Anissa Sutton

ALYZE ELYSE
UNLEASHING CREATIVE BRILLIANCE ACROSS FILM, MUSIC, AND ENTREPRENEURSHIP

In the realm of multi-talented creatives, Alyze Elyse stands out as an undeniable force. Her extraordinary abilities in screenwriting, songwriting, filmmaking, and acting have propelled her to remarkable heights in both the film and music industries. With the establishment of her independent production companies and her groundbreaking achievements in music, Alyze Elyse has created a fascinating world that continues to captivate audiences worldwide.

ESTABLISHING INDEPENDENT PRODUCTION COMPANIES:

Alyze Elyse's creative prowess has led her to establish her own independent production companies, Soul City Films and Alyze Elyse Productions. These ventures reflect her entrepreneurial spirit and desire for creative freedom. Through these companies, Alyze has been able to bring her artistic visions to life while maintaining full control over her projects.

CAPTIVATING AUDIENCES WITH FILM:

With an impressive filmography spanning diverse genres, Alyze Elyse has captivated audiences with her exceptional storytelling abilities. Works such as "Innocent" and "Going 4 Broke" have left a lasting impact on viewers, showcasing her ability to delve into various narratives and evoke powerful emotions.

MAKING HISTORY IN STREAMING AND FILM DISTRIBUTION:

Alyze Elyse has achieved a groundbreaking milestone as the first African American independent female filmmaker to amass over 100 million minutes streamed on Amazon Prime. This remarkable accomplishment highlights her impact on the industry and the powerful stories she tells through her films. Her success paved the way for future generations but also opens doors for underrepresented voices in the industry.

INDUCTION INTO THE WOMEN SONGWRITER HALL OF FAME:

Furthermore, in addition to her remarkable success in film, Alyze Elyse has also garnered recognition and accolades in the music industry. Her induction into the Women Songwriter Hall of Fame, alongside her chart-topping singles on both the Billboard and DRT charts, exemplifies her exceptional talent and contributions. As we eagerly anticipate the upcoming celebration on June 24th in Washington DC, Alyze will be celebrated among other accomplished songwriters, further solidifying her position as a versatile and accomplished artist.

ENTREPRENEURIAL VENTURES IN THE HAIR WIGS INDUSTRY:

In addition to her artistic pursuits, Alyze has recently embarked on a new entrepreneurial venture in the hair wigs industry. We're intrigued to learn more about this business endeavor and the motivations behind her decision to enter this particular market. By exploring her journey into entrepreneurship, we can understand how Alyze's passion for creativity extends beyond the realms of film and music, and how she seeks to make an impact in various industries.

In conclusion, Alyze Elyse's journey is a testament to her extraordinary talent and unwavering determination. From her establishment of independent production companies to her groundbreaking achievements, she continues to push boundaries and redefine what it means to be a multi-talented creative. As we anticipate her future endeavors and aspirations, Alyze Elyse stands as an inspiration to aspiring artists, filmmakers, and entrepreneurs, showing that with passion and dedication, the possibilities are limitless.

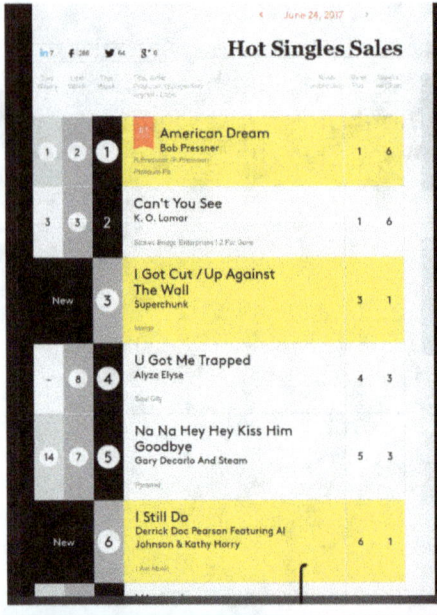

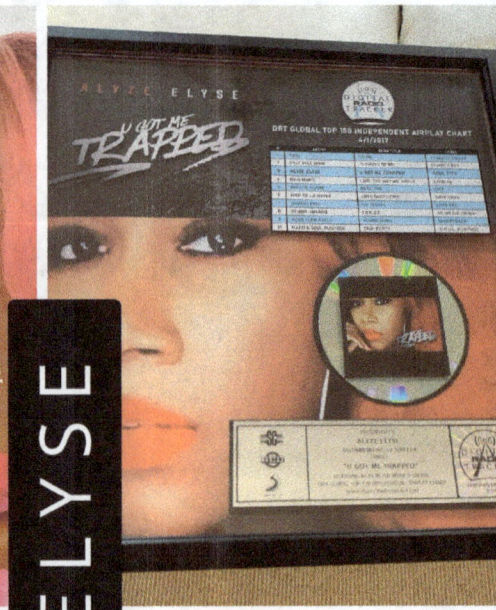

Alyze Elyse

"Going 4 Broke" is an uproarious comedy that takes audiences on a wild and hilarious rollercoaster ride filled with mayhem and madness. Written and directed by Alyze Elyse, this film combines humor, wit, and chaos to deliver a lighthearted yet thought-provoking story about the fear of financial struggle and the extraordinary lengths people will go to avoid it.

The story follows Seven and Tracy, two individuals on the brink of bankruptcy, as they embark on a series of outrageous adventures in their quest to secure the money they desperately need. Elyse's screenplay keeps the audience engaged from start to finish, as we witness their desperate antics unfold.

The film's comedic brilliance lies in the impeccable timing and chemistry between the lead actors. Their performances, along with Elyse's sharp direction, create an energetic and dynamic on-screen presence that keeps viewers hooked.

The supporting cast also deserves recognition for their contributions to the film's humor. Each character brings a unique flavor to the story, adding layers of comedy and complexity. From the eccentric neighbor to the quirky sidekick and formidable antagonist, every actor shines in their respective roles.

Visually, "Going 4 Broke" is a delightful feast for the eyes. The vibrant cinematography captures the chaos and energy of Seven and Tracy's misadventures, immersing the audience in their hilarious journey. The set designs and locations enhance the overall comedic tone, providing a colorful and lively backdrop for the unfolding madness.

While primarily a comedy, "Going 4 Broke" also touches on the universal fear of financial instability. It prompts viewers to reflect on their own anxieties and the absurd lengths they might go to avoid financial struggle. This underlying theme adds depth and resonance to the story, elevating it beyond a mere laugh-out-loud comedy.

In conclusion, Alyze Elyse's "Going 4 Broke" delivers laughs, surprises, and heartfelt moments in equal measure. With its talented cast, impeccable comedic timing, and a lively storyline, the film showcases Elyse's skill as both a writer and director. Whether you're in need of a good laugh or simply want to be entertained by a captivating comedy, "Going 4 Broke" is a must-watch. Prepare to be swept away by the mayhem and madness of Seven and Tracy's hilarious journey to avoid the one thing they fear most: going broke.

"Exposing the Covert Efforts to Control and Program the Black Community leaving viewers captivated and inspired to seek truth and social justice!"

"Exposing the Detrimental Impact: "NEUS" Unveils Covert Operations on the Black Community

NEUS" is an enthralling film directed by Jarrell Crump that fearlessly exposes the detrimental impact of covert operations on the black community. From its powerful opening line, "To understand the people, you have to understand the culture," the movie emphasizes the significance of cultural understanding in comprehending the challenges faced by marginalized communities. It delves into the insidious tactics employed to suppress the civil rights movement and hinder progress towards equality. Through its thought-provoking narrative, "NEUS" sheds light on the relentless efforts of covert operations to infiltrate, disrupt, and dismantle organizations and movements, revealing the hidden struggles faced by the black community.

Authentic Performances and Unwavering Commitment: The Power of "NEUS":

Under the skillful guidance of producer Alyze Elyse, "NEUS" comes to life as a testament to the unwavering commitment behind its creation. Elyse's dedication to shedding light on social issues shines through in the film, infusing it with purpose and authenticity. The talented cast, including Corey Jones and Terri Montrel, delivers outstanding performances that resonate with authenticity and emotion. Jones portrays his character's struggles with raw intensity, while Montrel adds depth and nuance to their role. Their exceptional acting enriches the narrative and captivates the audience, bringing the characters to life on screen.

Captivating Cinematography: Immersing Audiences in the Turmoil of "NEUS"

The film's captivating cinematography, expertly directed by Jarrell Crump, creates an immersive experience for the viewers. It vividly captures the turmoil and challenges faced by the characters, allowing the audience to emotionally connect with their journey. The visual elements enhance the storytelling, highlighting the impact of covert operations on the black community and emphasizing the urgency of seeking truth and justice. Through Crump's masterful direction, "NEUS" maintains a compelling and engaging pace, keeping the audience engaged from start to finish.

Resonant Music and Provocative Message: The Soundtrack of "NEUS" Amplifies the Revolution

The music in "NEUS" plays a pivotal role in enhancing the film's narrative and resonating with the audience. Featuring a brilliant hip-hop track and carefully selected songs, the music serves as a powerful complement to the storytelling. It heightens the emotional impact of the film, evoking visceral responses from viewers. By powerfully conveying its central message that the revolution will not be televised, "NEUS" urges audiences to question prevailing narratives and seek the underlying truth. The film serves as a reminder of the importance of vigilance in safeguarding democratic principles and fighting against systemic oppression.

MUSIC REVIEW 10 - 32

SOLFEGGIO FREQUENCY MUSIC A NATURAL PAINKILLER?

Every sound and every vibration has its own energy and own effect on the body and mind of living beings. The frequency of every sound works differently on the human body and now a recent study has proved that particular frequency music can heal many kinds of diseases and health-related issues.

This article is dedicated to healing music and Solfeggio music that how 174 Hz Solfeggio Frequency music can help relieve pain. Solfeggio music is often used for relieving pain, enhancing meditation's concentration, relieving stress, mind exercise and for yoga practice. That's why it is being called healing music as well.
Our nature has its own harmony and waves, which is roaming around the whole atmosphere. The human body is like an empty vessel and whenever it comes to get contact with these waves and energy, it has amazing effects on the body as well as mental status. Listening to a special kind of music on a special kind of frequency works as an anesthetic and a healer component which helps to generate the awakening mode and one can cure body pain easily and quickly.

Solfeggio music is one of the effective ways to reduce pain and develop a huge sense of love and courage inside you. 174 Hz Solfeggio music directly works on the chakras. Different chakras have different quality and according to spirituality human body contains 7 chakras. One can't be able to see these chakras directly but can be able to awake these chakras with deep Meditation and Pranayama. A person with an enlightened chakras is called an enlightened person which is quite rare.
Healing with sound and music is not a new phenomenon. From ancient time people used to listen to music for relaxation and better sleep.

Based on over 45 years of study and research on millions of people, the solfeggio frequency music is recognized for curing migraine, back pain, legs, and knee pain, enhancing courage and energy of the inner body. Let's take a closer look at some other benefits of solfeggio frequency music:

174 Hz Solfeggio frequency music is highly beneficial and effective for relieving pain. It appears as a natural anesthetic and helps to cure your sick aura around you.

BENEFITS OF SOLFEGGIO FREQUENCY MUSIC

74 Hz Solfeggio frequency music help to relieve back pain, foot pain, leg pain, lower back pain and migraine and stress.
It works like magic on your brain tissues and enhances the emotional power which encourages the sense of safety, love, and courage and helps to cure a person quickly.
174 Hz solfeggio music is the finest source for better concentration level.
174 Hz frequency music contains different nodes and background tones which directly affects the chakras and develops the healing power and energy that makes you feel better.
174 Hz solfeggio frequency music is an excellent way to reduce emotional pain as well. The people who have lost someone or forgot to live happily can get the positive results with this music mode.

THE HEALING ABILITY OF 174HZ MUSIC

Many skepticals ignore the benefits and effects of solfeggio frequency music.

But a recent study at Harvard University has been proved that the patients listening to the solfeggio frequency music were recovering fast and their mental status was far better than non-listener.

174Hz music especially helps in relieving pain as it works like a natural anesthesia and doctors were amazed to find an important fact during surgery that those patients who were listening to healing music during surgery needed less anesthetic dose and they felt less pain during and after surgery.

Listen to OM Mantra Chants at a very low 174 Hz frequency.

OM – The Sound That Reverberates across the universe. The Sound which brings beauty to every cell of our body.

AUM or OM, no matter how you write it, its the inner sound of cosmos. And we have combined it with powerful Solfeggio frequency which is known for its benefits in Pain Relief.

Editions L.A.

DIGITAL CREATIVE AGENCY

We Transform Your Vision Into Creative Results

Editions L.A. is a full-service agency based in Los Angeles. Our company is a collective of amazing people striving to build delightful services
We believe that is all about getting your message across clearly and with a "Wow!" thrown in for good measure.

Our Awesome Services

Branding

We build, style and tone your brand identity from the ground up.
We rebrand established bands, brands or businesses.

Merchandise Store
Website design and E-Commerce
Website updates

Digital Marketing

CD Cover | Banners | Logo design | Flyers | Brochures | Leaflets | Print ads | Magazine covers & artworks
Facebook / twitter / instagram / youtube artworks
| Book cover
Infographics | Icon Design |
| TshirtsProduct Labels | Presentation slides
Corporate graphics
Professional photo editing & enhancing
Redesign existing elements
YouTube Optimization and Monetization
Youtube Video Editing
Lyric Video and Advertising Design.

Publishing

BOOK COVER DESIGN
EBOOK FORMATTING SERVICES
and distribution on major platforms
(Amazon, Barnes & Nobles..)

Tell us about your dream and we will make it true!

Editions L.A.
7210 Jordan Avenue Suite B42, Canoga Park, California 91303, United States
info@edtions-la.com
Website: www.editions-la.com

EMPOWERING SONGS

WHETHER YOU'RE LOOKING FOR SOME ENCOURAGEMENT OR JUST NEED TO BE REMINDED OF THE STRONG AND POWERFUL WOMAN YOU ARE, TURN UP YOUR VOLUME AND GET READY BECAUSE THESE ARE SOME OF THE BEST GIRL POWER SONGS EVER...

"The Man" Taylor Swift
Taylor Swift shines a big light on the double standards between men and women in this song from her album Lover.
Most empowering lyric: "Wondering if I'd get there quicker / If I was a man / And I'm so sick of them coming at me again / 'Cause if I was a man / Then I'd be the man"

"Who Says" - Selena Gomez & The Scene
All that matters is that you love you despite what anyone says.
Most empowering lyric: "But who are you to judge / When you're a diamond in the rough / I'm sure you got some things / You'd like to change about yourself / But when it comes to me / I wouldn't want to be anybody else"

"Mother's Daughter" - Miley Cyrus
Miley lets us all know that there's power in freedom.
Most empowering lyric: "Oh my God, she got the power / Oh, look at her, she got the power / So-so, so don't f*ck with my freedom"

"Hey Girl" - Lady Gaga and Florence Welsh
Hey girls, we should always have each other's backs!
Most empowering lyric: "Hey girl, hey girl / We can make it easy if we lift each other / Hey girl, hey girl / We don't need to keep on one-in' up another / Hey girl, hey girl / Hey girl, hey girl / If you lose your way / Just know that I got you"

"Formation" - Beyoncé
Like the Queen B says, we've gotta work hard to get what's ours.
Most empowering lyric: "I go hard, I go hard / Get what's mine, take what's mine / I'm a star, I'm a star / 'Cause I slay, slay"

EMPOWERING BOOKS

EMPOWERING SELF-HELP BOOKS EVERY WOMAN SHOULD READ

'More Than Enough' by Elaine Welteroth

Elaine Welteroth is here to tell you that you're more than enough. In this memoir-slash-manifesto, the 'Project Runway' judge and former 'Teen Vogue' Editor in Chief takes readers inside her own barrier-breaking life and career while providing lessons on race, identity,

Untamed' by Glennon Doyle

If you haven't read Glennon Doyle's 'Untamed' by now, do yourself a favor and order a copy immediately. In the book, Doyle takes readers through her journey to living a truly authentic life that will inspire you to do the same. And, remember, "We can do hard things."

'Pofessional Troublemaker' by Luvvie Ajayi Jones

Imposter syndrome? Never heard of her. Luvvie Ajayi Jones is here to help you tackle fear both in your professional and personal life through her signature humor and refreshing honesty.

'Own It' by Diane von Furstenberg

Keep this pocket-sized A-Z guide to life from the one and only Diane von Furstenberg on your desk for whenever you're in need of a pick-me-up.

'Believe It' by Jamie Kern Lima

Jamie Kern Lima, founder of IT Cosmetics and the first female CEO of a L'Oréal brand, shares her empowering story of navigating the beauty industry's impossible standards while helping you overcome any feelings of self-doubt that may be holding you back in your own life.

THE FUTURE IS FEMALE

EMPOWERING MOVIES

OUR FAVORITE FILMS THAT PUT WOMEN FRONT AND CENTER

'Promising Young Woman'
Trigger warning: Sexual assault. Director Emerald Fennell and actress Carey Mulligan confront rape culture, toxic masculinity, and trauma in Promising Young Woman. Mulligan plays a barista-vigilante out for vengeance for the college campus rape of her best friend. The film will enrage you, but it is also incredibly empowering and cathartic.

'The Color Purple'
Alice Walker's Pulitzer Prize-winning novel materialized on screen in 1985 and became an iconic feminist film that withstands the tests of time. Whoopi Goldberg plays Celie, a Black southern women who has suffered (and survived) years of abuse and finds strength within herself and female friends.

'Moana"
Brave heroine? Check. Adventure? Check. Hilarious sidekick? Also check. Lin-Manuel Miranda soundtrack? YOU BETCHA. Moana is the modern Disney hero we needed, one who is tough and empowered. Bonus points that there is no pointless love interest in this movie! Don't care if this one is for kids, we will be watching (and rewatching) for years to come.

'Bombshell'
In this ripped-from-the-headlines flick, Charlize Theron and Nicole Kidman, playing Fox News anchors Megyn Kelly and Gretchen Carlson, work together to expose expose FOX CEO Roger Ailes of sexual harassment. Exceptionally good facial prosthetics aside, Theron, Kidman, and Margo Robbie (who plays a fictional character) give a, ahem, bombshell performance.

'Thelma & Louise'
There's no greater movie about sisterhood than Thelma & Louise—a landmark feminist film about two women on a road trip. Watch it with your friends for fun, then analyze it with your friends for even more fun.
(And FYI, this film launched Brad Pitt's entire career, so you're welcome, Brad Pitt.)

ANEESSA
MICHAEL B. SUTTON

I FOUND MYSELF IN YOU

OUT NOW

WWW.THESOUNDOFLA.COM

*Smooth Jazz Love Song
for An Essential Romantic Playlist
Capturing the joyful essence of
what it feels like
to love and be loved!*

B. CARTER MAN
FIESTA

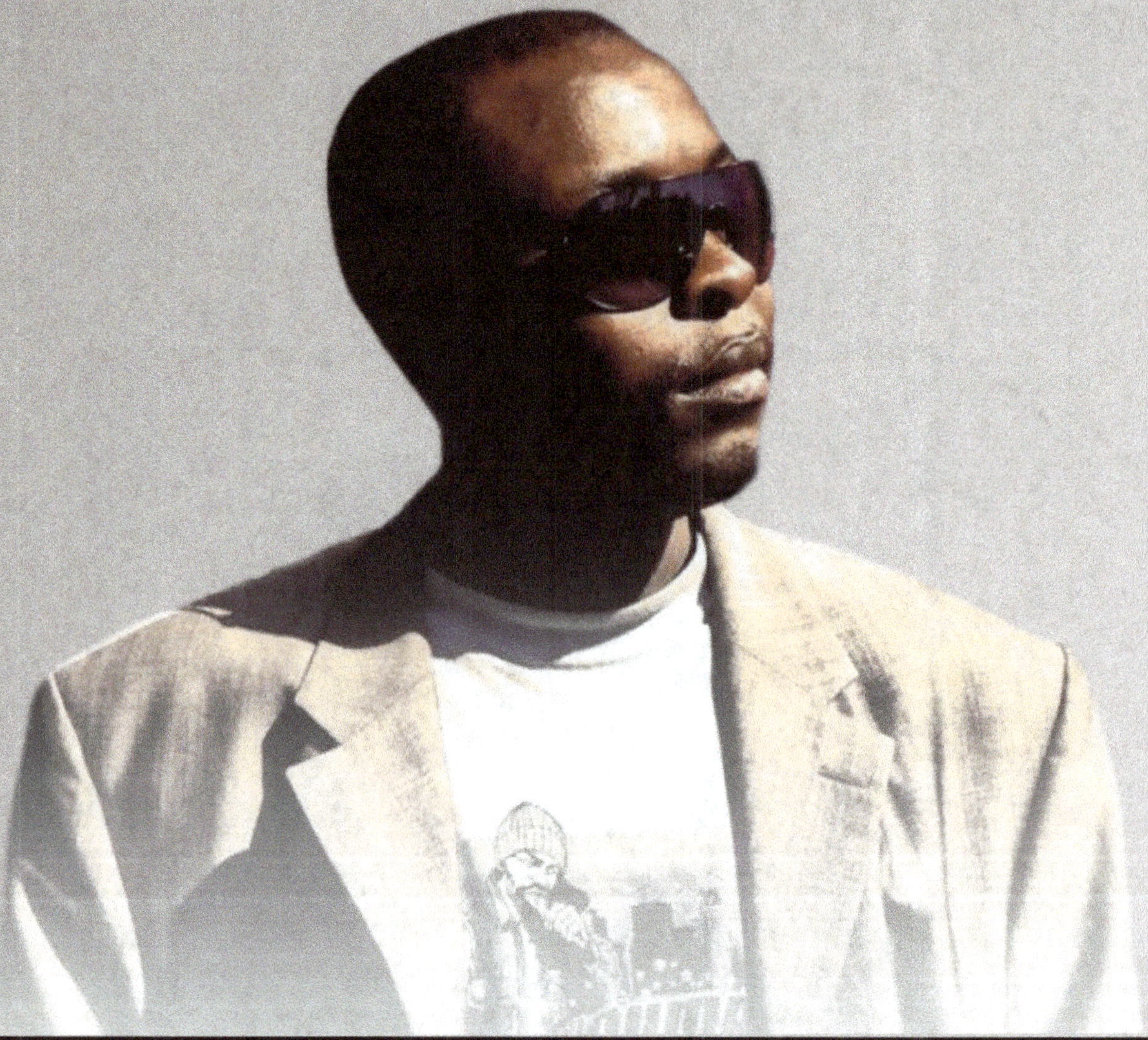

Get ready to party with B. Carter Kaya Man's
latest hip-hop single "Fiesta"!
Let loose and move to the beat with catchy lyrics and an energetic rhythm!

    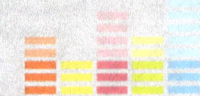  

PRE-ORDER NOW
AND JOIN THE "FIESTA"
ON MARCH 24TH!

BEAUTY 20 - 34

3 TIPS TO
Stay Beautiful

01
TONER MIXED WITH FACIAL OIL

So that the skin is always shiny, mix moisturizing toner with two drops of facial oil

02
ALWAYS WEAR SUNSCREEN

Sunscreen to protect the skin from red rashes due to excessive UV exposure

03
HYDRATE FROM WITHIN BY DRINKING

Drinking large amounts of water can keep the skin moist from within

FOLLOW US @pumpitupmagazine

FASHION

3 SYLE TIPS TO
LOOK YOUNGER

01
GO MONOCHROME:
A way to look super sophisticated
You will never go wrong with wearing all one color!

02
ANKLE-LENGTH DENIM:
Any jeans that hit right at the ankle are always the best kind of denim!

03
WHEN IN DOUBT, TUCK IN YOUR SHIRT:
Whether it's a half tuck or a full tuck, this look will definitely make you feel more youthful and slimmer

FOLLOW US @pumpitupmagazine

WEST END ORGANIX

Ageless Beauty, Organic Health

BLACK SEED OIL

HEALTHY IMMUNE SYSTEM
INFLAMMATORY RESPONSE

www.westendorganix.com

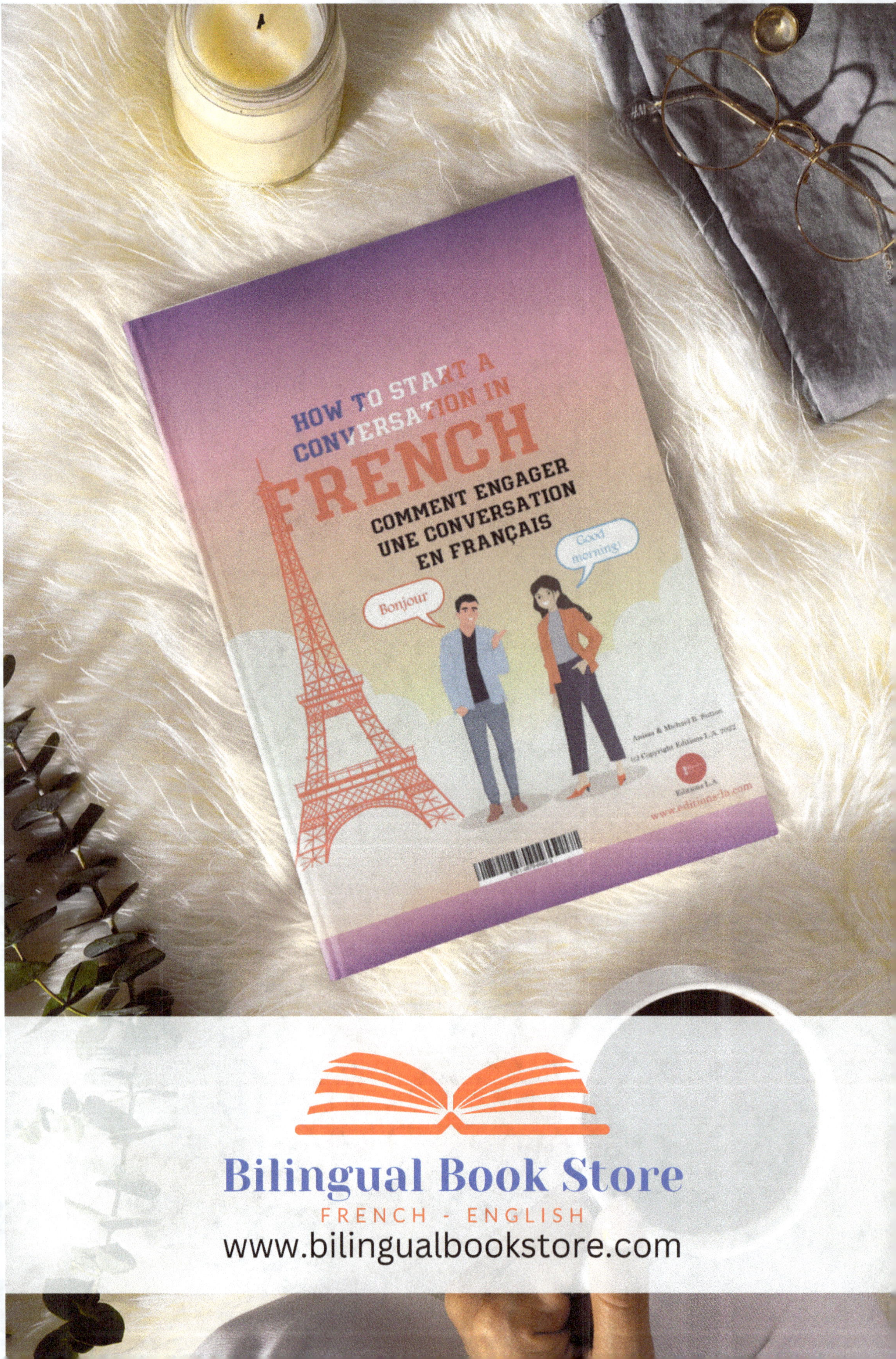

Bilingual Book Store

FRENCH - ENGLISH

www.bilingualbookstore.com

COUPLE'S WORKOUTS:
A BONDING EXPERIENCE FOR FITNESS AND RELATIONSHIPS

Working out together can be a fun and effective way to bond with your significant other while also improving your physical health. Not only will you be able to support and motivate each other, but you'll also have the opportunity to create new memories and strengthen your relationship. Here are some ideas for couple's workouts that you can try together:

Outdoor activities: Going for a walk, hike, or bike ride together can be a great way to enjoy the beautiful outdoors while getting some exercise. Try to find a new trail or park to explore each week to keep things fresh and exciting.

Group fitness classes: Trying a new workout together, such as yoga, Pilates, or dance, can be a fun and unique bonding experience. Not only will you be able to challenge each other physically, but you'll also have the opportunity to learn and grow together.

Home workouts: If you're short on time or don't want to go to the gym, consider doing a workout together at home. There are many online resources available with at-home workouts that can be done with minimal equipment.

Competitive games: Incorporating some friendly competition into your workout can make it even more enjoyable. Try playing a game of basketball, tennis, or even a friendly race to add an extra challenge and some fun.

Weight lifting: If you're both looking to build strength, consider lifting weights together. Not only will you be able to spot each other and keep each other safe, but you'll also have the opportunity to push each other to new limits.

In conclusion, incorporating physical activity into your relationship can be a great way to bond with your significant other while also improving your health. So, whether you're trying a new fitness class, exploring the outdoors, or lifting weights together, make sure to have fun and enjoy each other's company. Remember, the journey is as important as the destination, so be patient, trust the process, and enjoy the ride.

4 WEEKS FULL BODY WORKOUT CHALLENGE

Week 1 — Focus on your form

Sunday	Lower Body
Monday	Upper Body
Tuesday	Cross Training
Wednesday	Total Body
Thursday	Abs
Friday	Cross Training
Saturday	Rest Time

Week 2 — Go for more reps

Sunday	Lower Body
Monday	Upper Body
Tuesday	Cross Training
Wednesday	Total Body
Thursday	Abs
Friday	Cross Training
Saturday	Rest Time

Week 3 — Try a new cross-training workout

Sunday	Lower Body
Monday	Upper Body
Tuesday	Cross Training
Wednesday	Total Body
Thursday	Abs
Friday	Cross Training
Saturday	Rest Time

Week 4 — Complete and Extra Round

Sunday	Lower Body
Monday	Upper Body
Tuesday	Cross Training
Wednesday	Total Body
Thursday	Abs
Friday	Cross Training
Saturday	Rest Time

Pump it up

FROM WALKING TO RUNNING
4 Weeks Fit Challenge

	1st Week	2nd Week	3rd Week	4th Week
SUN	5 Mins Steady Run 1 Mins Walk Repat 3x	5 Mins Steady Run 1 Mins Walk Repat 4x	5 Mins Steady Run 2 Mins Walk Repat 5x	5 Mins Steady Run 2 Mins Walk Repat 6x
MON	7 Mins Steady Run 1 Mins Walk Repat 3x	8 Mins Steady Run 2 Mins Walk Repat 4x	10 Mins Steady Run 3 Mins Walk Repat 5x	12 Mins Steady Run 3 Mins Walk Repat 6x
TUE	REST DAY	REST DAY	REST DAY	REST DAY
WED	7 Mins Steady Run 1 Mins Walk Repat 3x	Speed Intervals	20 Mins Progression Run	Body Weight Strength Workout
THU	15 Mins Easy Run or Walk	15 Progression Run	Speed Intervals	Speed Intervals
FRI	REST DAY	REST DAY	REST DAY	REST DAY
SAT	Speed Intervals	Body Weight Strength Workout	Body Weight Strength Workout	30 Mins Progression Run

WELLNESS

"Crossword puzzles help human brain function."

Many people believe this statement, but can't support it with research and trusted sources; that is, until now! The health benefits of crossword puzzles are not limited to cognitive function, though. Here are the five primary yet surprising health benefits of crossword puzzles.

CROSSWORDS DELAY MEMORY LOSS AND HELP ALLEVIATE DEMENTIA.

When most people ask if crosswords are good for brain health, they're most likely wondering if crosswords help strengthen memory. As this study found, solving crossword puzzles later in life delayed memory decline by 2.5 years in those who had developed dementia. Previous education of the participants was not a factor in the results.

In similar studies, researchers found that these benefits help those who are already at risk for Alzheimer's or dementia the most. In other words, if you're at risk for Alzheimer's or dementia, you may benefit from regularly enjoying crossword puzzles.

CROSSWORDS PRESERVE MEMORY, COGNITIVE FUNCTION, AND OVERALL BRAIN STRENGTH.

In another study, researchers found that those who regularly do crosswords have the brain strength of someone 10 years younger than themselves. Scientists and researchers have also found that solvers will get the most cognitive benefits of crossword puzzles by consistently challenging themselves. You can challenge yourself even more with crosswords by:

Increasing the size and/or difficulty of the puzzle regularly.
Timing yourself as you solve the crossword.
Using fewer materials to help you solve.
Solving foreign language crosswords.

YOU CAN STRENGTHEN YOUR VOCABULARY AND SPELLING THROUGH CROSSWORDS.

Crosswords strengthen the vocabulary and spelling of students and adults alike. A larger vocabulary, in turn, can increase your processing speed and your abstract thinking. This kind of mental boost can lead to greater professional success, as well.

And crosswords don't strengthen vocabulary and spelling alone. Solving crosswords can also boost your knowledge of trivia, which has similar cognitive benefits.

SOLVING CROSSWORDS AS A GROUP STRENGTHENS SOCIAL BONDS.

By solving crosswords with friends and family, you'll strengthen your social bonds through fun and conversation. Social connections help you live longer and improve your quality of life. More importantly, a lack of social connection is a greater detriment to health than issues such as obesity and smoking. In other words, inviting your friends over for a crossword-solving party could have just as much of an impact on your health as exercise.

CROSSWORDS ALLEVIATE ANXIETY, WHICH WILL IMPROVE YOUR MOOD.

There are still ways to achieve emotional health benefits from crosswords as a solo solver. For example, more intellectually stimulating exercises might improve anxiety. A study found that people with anxiety were more successful at tasks requiring concentration – such as crosswords – than activities most people consider more "relaxing." This finding relates to the idea that stress beats anxiety by redirecting nervous energy to a task that requires problem-solving.

VEGETABLES Word Search

Circle words in the puzzle below

```
E T Y A M A C
L E T T U C E
E P E A S E L
E T C L H T E
K K O K R A R
C A R R O T Y
C O N I O N P
Z F B Y M A U
```

mushroom   okra   lettuce   yam
carrot   celery   peas   onion
           leek   corn

3 WORDS YOU SEE
= PERSONALITY TRAITS

A	C	K	F	B	A	K
V	U	I	N	Y	M	H
B	O	N	S	Q	B	O
A	M	D	R	N	I	N
S	I	N	C	E	R	E
H	X	S	A	M	I	S
F	U	N	N	Y	O	T
U	O	S	Y	K	U	A
L	A	Z	Y	L	S	C

BOOST LIVE STREAM SUCCESS:
A GUIDE TO ENHANCING SOUND, APPEARANCE, AND PROMOTION

MAKE IT SOUND GOOD

Level up your streaming game with superior audio quality. Connect external mics like AT2020USB+, Apogee HypeMic, or AKG Lyra to your phone for studio-grade sound. Use a pop filter to minimize mic popping, wear headphones for monitoring, and consider a wind shield for outdoor streams. Explore dedicated microphones, audio interfaces, and mixers for optimal results. Enhance your sound further with production software like iZotope Nectar, featuring highpass filtering, gating, compression, and EQ. Stand out in the competitive streaming world by delivering exceptional audio that captivates your audience. Upgrade your setup and make your streams sound professional and engaging.

MAKE IT LOOK GOOD

Avoid distractions in your videos by tidying up the background. Consider what your audience will see before you begin. Utilize virtual backgrounds in apps like Zoom for a versatile setting. Create a DIY green screen using light-green poster boards for an economical solution. Invest in a smartphone or tablet stand for optimal positioning, offering flexibility and professional angles.

LIGHTING IS IMPORTANT

Make sure that people can see your face — that's how they connect with you. Pull out those Christmas lights and string them around. Turn down the background lights. Put a soft light in front of you and maybe a halo light above and behind you.

CHECK YOUR INTERNET CONNECTION

If you are wired, then you should be fine. If wireless (either Wi-Fi or cell service), double-check your connection speed before you start. Find the place that offers the most robust connection (the most bars). I just live streamed a wedding from a field last weekend, and the 4G connection was weak. Fortunately, I had a mobile hot spot that I was able to connect to, and we made it work. If the internet connection is too slow or inadequate for streaming, then it will frustrate you and annoy your viewers..

TEST IT BEFORE YOU START

Have a friend watch and listen to a test stream before you go live. Don't be the artist who goes live and says, "I don't know if you guys can see me or hear me yet…" Think of the test run like you would a recorded rehearsal. Look at it objectively and make sure you are represented the way you want to appear — look, sound, demeanor, banter, background. Review it yourself and fix anything you don't like about it before you go live.

PROMOTE IT AHEAD OF TIME

Let people know what time you'll be doing it. Determine when your viewers will be available and pick a time during that window. On the weekends, people flip through their feeds most hours of the day. During the week, however, most people will check their socials around lunch between 1–3PM ET and after dinner around 7:30PM ET to bedtime. Give them enough time to put it on their calendars and reserve the time. Even the best stream will underperform if people don't know about it.

THE STEPLADDER APPROACH
Helping children with anxiety through gradual exposure.

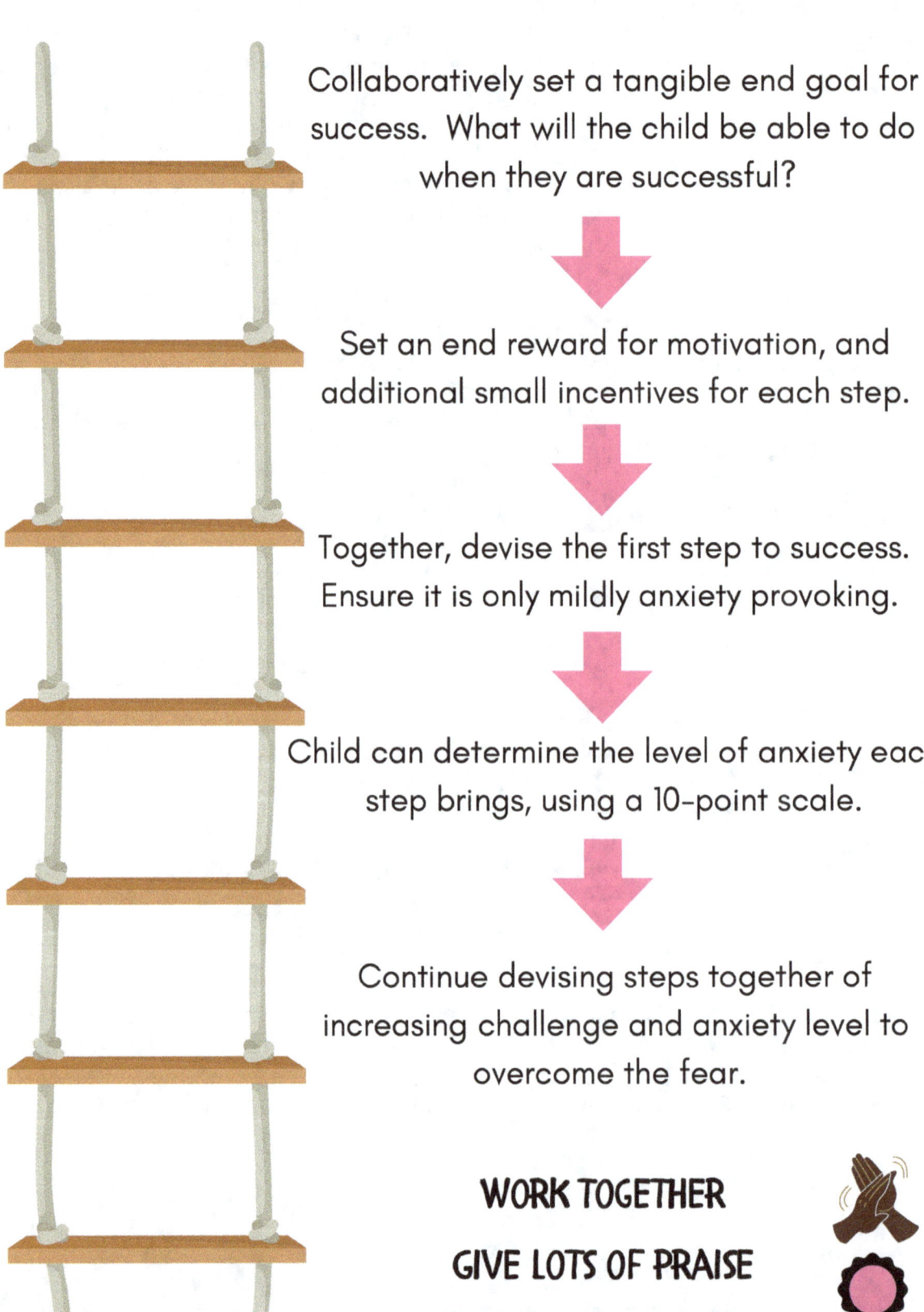

Collaboratively set a tangible end goal for success. What will the child be able to do when they are successful?

⬇

Set an end reward for motivation, and additional small incentives for each step.

⬇

Together, devise the first step to success. Ensure it is only mildly anxiety provoking.

⬇

Child can determine the level of anxiety each step brings, using a 10-point scale.

⬇

Continue devising steps together of increasing challenge and anxiety level to overcome the fear.

WORK TOGETHER

GIVE LOTS OF PRAISE

REWARDS AS INCENTIVES

How anxious are you?

OVER THE LAST 2 WEEKS, HOW OFTEN HAVE YOU BEEN BOTHERED BY THE FOLLOWING PROBLEMS	Not at all	Several days	More than half the days	Nearly every day
Feeling nervous, anxious or on edge	0	1	2	3
Not being able to stop or control worrying	0	1	2	3
Worrying too much about different things	0	1	2	3
Trouble relaxing	0	1	2	3
Feeling afraid, as if something awful might happen	0	1	2	3

What your total score means Your total score is a guide to how severe your anxiety disorder may be: •0 to 4 = mild anxiety •5 to 9 = moderate anxiety •10 to 14 = moderately severe anxiety •15 to 21 = severe anxiety If your score is 10 or higher, or if you feel that anxiety is affecting your daily life, call your doctor

Are you a songwriter or composer struggling to protect your work and releases?
Well Bernie Capodici has done all the work for you in his new book
"Modern Recording Artist Handbook, How To Guide Simplified"

Only $12.95

MUST READ FOR INDEPENDENT ARTISTS

 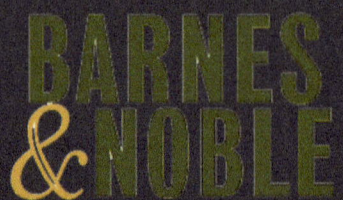

KINDLE $9.99 - HARDCOVER $22.95 - PAPERBACK $12.95

www.ingramcontent.com/pod-product-compliance
Lightning Source LLC
Chambersburg PA
CBHW080901010526
44118CB00015B/2232